TWENTY-FIVE CENTS.

# WAR LYRICS:

BY

## W. A. DEVON,

AUTHOR OF

"RED MARK," "HAROLD," &c., &c.

---

NEW YORK:
SINCLAIR TOUSEY, 121 NASSAU STREET.
1864.

# WAR LYRICS:

BY

W. A. DEVON,

AUTHOR OF

"RED MARK," "HAROLD," &c., &c.

---

NEW YORK:

SINCLAIR TOUSEY, 121 NASSAU STREET.

1864.

*Second Edition.*

# CONTENTS.

# WAR LYRICS.

# WAR LYRICS.

——oo——

## THE WATCHER.

I

Fair Madeline sat in the oriel pane,
  Through the light of the long Summer days,
She sighed not, she wept not, she did not complain,
  Although fading away from our gaze,
Her meek dreamy eyes were bent far away,
  And her brow wore a spiritual light,
Her little hands clasped, like saints when they pray,
  And the rose of her cheek had turned white!
She spoke not, she wept not, she did not complain,
But wistfully gazed through the wide oriel pane,
Repeating at times to her heart this wild strain—
"Oh, Father of Heaven! once more let him come,
  To lighten the weight of my sorrow,
That he may but learn from my lips I repent,
  But surely he'll come on the morrow!"

II

She sat and she watched the bright golden hair'd
    dawn,
  As it rose in the orient fair,
She watched her pale sisters the meek stars with-
    drawn,
  And the Sun's ruby light flood the air;
She watched the mild eve, as with wide-spreading
    palms,
  And starry sprent garments of gray!

As she seemed to repeat sweet spiritual psalms
 In the ear of the faint dying day!
She spoke not, she wept not, she did not complain,
But wistfully gazed through the wide oriel pane,
Repeating at times to her heart this wild strain—
"Oh, Father of Heaven! once more let him come,
 To lighten the weight of my sorrow,
That he may but learn from my lips I repent,
 But surely he'll come on the morrow!"

III

She watched till the day had been swallowed by night,
 Till the moon and her bright starry train
Had blossomed and bloomed into flowrets of light,
 Till the dawn had devoured them again!
She watched in the sunlight the bright dancing leaves,
 Heard the grasshopper piping his blast;
Heard the young swallows twitter under the eaves,
 Saw the rosey-lipp'd Summer dance past!
She spoke not, she wept not, she did not complain,
But wistfully gazed through the wide oriel pane,
Repeating at times to her heart this wild strain—
"Oh, Father of Heaven! once more let him come,
 To lighten the weight of my sorrow,
That he may but learn from my lips I repent,
 But surely he'll come on the morrow"

IV

She watched the brown Autumn amid the fields stand,
 With his ripe fruits and blood-tinged leaves;
Then pass, like a spirit of light through the land,
 Sprinkling it o'er with bright yellow sheaves;

She watched through the gloom of the bleak Winter
time,
When the Sun scarcely peered through the cloud,
When nature lay dead, and the white frozen rime,
And the lily-white snow was her shroud!
She wept not, she spoke not, she did not complain,
But wistfully gazed through the wide oriel pane,
Repeating at times to her heart this wild strain—
"Oh, Father of Heaven! once more let him come,
To lighten the weight of my sorrow,
That he may but learn from my lips I repent,
But surely he'll come on the morrow!"

V

Fair Madeline rose from her snowy-white bed,
And gone from her face was her sorrow,
"He's coming! he's coming!" she merrily said,
And life from the thought she did borrow!
She decked her in robes of bright silken sheen,
With a wreath of rich gems in her hair,
And daintily sat, like a bright fairy queen,
And all day down the valley did stare!
She sighed not, she wept not, she did not complain,
But silently sat in the wide oriel pane,
Repeating at times to herself the sweet strain—
"Oh, Father, I thank Thee! my love has returned,
To lighten the weight of my sorrow,
And to learn from my lips how deep I repent—
I dreamt he would come on this morrow!"

VI

The day wore apace, till the gray, blushing eve
Brought the clatter of hoofs to the gate;
When a war-battered soldier stood begging for leave
On the fair Madeline for to wait.
"I come, lovely maid, from the red field of strife,

Where the bravest of soldiers was slain,
He begged me to come, with his last breath of life,
And bear you this message of pain!"
She sighed not, she wept not, she did not complain,
But blankly she stared through the wide oriel pane,
And slowly repeated this heart-breaking strain:
"Oh, God! can it be, that he'll ne'er come again,
To lighten the weight of my sorrow;
And to learn from my lips how deep I repent—
Oh, God! is there never a morrow!"

VII

As the bronzed soldier spoke he brushed off a tear—
"How he loved you, you never can know;—
He was kind, he was brave, and void of all fear
When he dashed in the midst of the foe;
Oh, God, how he smote them, both root, limb and branch,
As if Azrail rode on his breath!
And rushed with the roar of a wild avalanche,
In the red-flaming throat of grim Death!"
She sighed not, she wept not, she did not complain,
But blankly she gazed through the wide oriel pane,
And slowly repeated the heart-breaking strain:
"Oh, God! can it be that he'll ne'er come again,
To lighten the weight of my sorrow,
And learn from my lips how deep I repent—
Oh, Lord! is there never a morrow!"

VIII

As they silently watched the dark shadows steal,
When the soldier had taken his leave,
They saw the red sunset, like God's golden seal,
Brightly stamped on the edge of the eve!
They silently sat in the gathering gloom,
With a feeling of wonder and dread;

At length, with soft footsteps, they crossed the dark
room,
But the fair Madeline she was dead!
She sighed not, she breathed not, she did not complain,
But blankly she stared through the wide oriel pane,
Their lips now repeating her sad, mournful strain:
"Oh, God! can it be, that she'll ne'er come again,
To lighten the weight of our sorrow;
Yet tearful we thank Thee, her soul is at rest
In the light of Eternity's morrow!"

## GETTYSBURG.*

I

Raise the marble trophy high,
Raise it for no cunning lie,
Raise a shrine of Victory
On the field of Gettysburg.

II

Gather up their precious dust,
Now their country's sacred trust,
Lay it with the brave and just
Who repose at Gettysburg.

III

Where our country's heroes sleep,
Where the nation comes to weep,
Tears of sorrow, dark and deep,
O'er the dead at Gettysburg.

IV

Where our noble soldiers fell,
'Mid the battle's fearful swell,

* This poem was written expressly for the N. Y. Dispatch, and appears by their permission.

Rolling like the waves of hell,
  O'er the field of Gettysburg.

V

Let the page of history say,
How they fought day after day,
We come our last respects to pay
  To our dead at Gettysburg.

VI

Here the mother's heart shall yearn
O'er the Nation's funeral cairn,
Weeping for her noble bairn,
  Sleeping still at Gettysburg.

VII

Fathers here, with manly tears,
Shall wander i' their childless years,
And o'er the dust his heart reveres,
  Weep the lost at Gettysburg.

VIII

Widowed hearts shall sadly mourn,
O'er their country's grateful urn,
For the loved who'll ne'er return
  From the grave at Gettysburg.

IX

Orphan lips shall learn to name
This sad spot, so dear to Fame,
Where the sire from whom they came
  Sleeps serene at Gettysburg.

X

Brothers brave and sisters fair,
In memory will oft repair,
Breathing forth a mournful prayer
  O'er the dust at Gettysburg.

XI

While the Nation's heart shall keep
All their memories treasured deep,
For they died that we might reap
  Th' glory won at Gettysburg.

XII

Weave a laurel for each brow,
Hang it as a trophy now,
Where the mourning pageants bow
  On the field of Gettysburg.

XIII

Future ages yet unborn,
Will tell of that bright July morn,
Where, amidst the trampled corn,
  We met the foe at Gettysburg.

XIV

How the charging squadrons dashed,
How the gleaming bayonets flashed,
How the thundering cannon crashed
  Those three days at Gettysburg.

XV

How the foeman's deadly yell
Rose above the cannon's swell,
Ringing out a fearful knell
  For the slain at Gettysburg.

XVI

While throughout the bloody fray,
Th' deadly roll of musketry
Rained through all the summer's day,
  Tears of blood at Gettysburg.

XVII

As Atlantic waves are broke
On some wild and jutting rock,

So they stood the fearful shock,
All those days at Gettysburg.

XVIII

Still they sought the battle's breath,
Where they feel a bleeding swath
'Neath the scythe of grinning Death,
Who reaped the field of Gettysburg.

XIX

Who may paint that crimson flood,
That red sea of human blood,
Where unmoved our heroes stood
In the storm of Gettysburg?

XX

All unmurmuring was it borne,
From the bright-eyed summer's morn,
Till the moon's clear silver horn
Lit the dead at Gettysburg.

XXI

On Golgotha's fearful mound,
Where the dead lay strewn around,
In the sleep of death profound,
On the field of Gettysburg.

XXII

Thus we lay them side by side,
Where the gallant heroes died,
In their triumph and their pride,
On the field of Gettysburg.

XXIII

Thus we leave them still and gory,
On the crimson field of glory;
Richest theme of song and story,
That red field of Gettysburg.

## THE WIDOW'S MITE.

I

Columbia! oh, Columbia! my own, my native land,
I love thee with a peerless love that few can understand;
They say I'm old and feeble now, and near the sunny strand,
But still the more thou'rt dear to me, my own, my native land!

II

One by one the limbs of life have long been torn away,
And lonely I am left to stand in life's declining day;
My husband and my children dear have reached the blessed shore,
And here in patient hope I wait to join my loved once more!

III

I have one boy—one only boy—the bravest and the best,
The only stay on all the earth whereon my hopes can rest;
But still my dear, my native land, though bitter is the cup,
With all a martyr's thrilling joy, I freely give him up!

IV

To battle for the dear old land of childhood's happy day,
Ere she had learned to curse her own, or be the rebel's prey;
To stand within the breach of death and smite the traitor foe,
Who dares to rend thy bleeding heart and lay thy glory low!

V

God only knows how dear he is, the poor old widow's boy,
The light of my declining steps, my only hope and joy;
But dear as this last link must be unto a mother's heart,
Were he as dear a thousand times, I'd freely with him part!

VI

'Tis said the good Lord smiling viewed the widow's mite though small,
For she into the treasury cast her living—aye, her all;
So thus I cast my widow's mite into thy rifled store,
And were it mine a thousand times I'd give it o'er and o'er!

VII

Into thy heated crucible I cast my mite of ore,
Well knowing in my inmost heart it shall be mine no more;
Yet still dear land, though lone and old, I fill a nameless grave,
I'd freely give my life, my all, thy heritage to save!

VIII

Columbia! oh, Columbia! my own, my native land,
I love thee with a peerless love that few can understand;
They say I'm old and feeble now, and near the sunny strand,
Yet still the more thou'rt dear to me, my own, my native land!

## THE WIDOW TO HER SON.

I

Go forth, go forth, my gallant boy, unto the field of strife,
And may the God of battles spare thy young and noble life;
But ever in the bleeding gap be foremost in the fight,
And thus thy noble battle-cry, "May God defend the right!"

II

I know, I know, my gallant boy, the bare suspicion pains,
For not a drop of coward blood can flow within thy veins;
Thy lips are set, thy cheek burns red, with nature's crimson tide;
I spoke, but from that stainless stream, a mother's love and pride!

III

Go forth, go forth, my noble boy, on war's red burning path,
And snatch the wreath of glory from the bleeding fangs of death,
And strike to earth the rebel horde, who dare to raise a hand
Against fair freedom's holy shrine, our dear, our native land!

IV

Go! take this sword, the noblest gift a mother ever gave!
Go! win the victor's laurel wreath, or fill a hero's grave!

You see I weep—my own brave boy—from pride,
far more thăn pain,
That I've been spared one noble arm our birthright
to maintain.

V

Go! battle for that grand old flag, that flaunting
floats on high,
The symbol of a world's hope, for which you dare to
die,
Nor suffer one bright starry gem to leave that shining
field,
Whilst thou canst fire a rifle ball or this bright falchion
wield!

VI

Go! son of mine, in valor's front, and when the battle's
blare,
With all its hissing storm of death, is crashing every-
where,
When charging squadron's madly dash down on the
solid squaro,
Amidst the deafening roar of guns, whose thunder fill
the air!

VII

Think in that hour, that fearful hour, when stoutest
hearts might fail,
That then a mother's earnest prayer's may with the
Lord prevail,
That he may be thy sun and shield in battle's evil
day,
And bring thee off, my noble boy, all harmless from
the fray!

VIII

Go forth, go forth! my noble boy, unto the field of
strife,

And may the God of battle's spare thy young and
noble life,
But ever in the bleeding gap be foremost in the fight,
And thus thy noble battle cry, "May God defend the
right!"

## THE PICKET.

I

Away, by the swampy Pamunky,
'Mid the silence and gloom of the night;
While the moon through the black driving clouds,
Shed fragments of quivering light;
Revealing the far away mountains,
And dark rolling river before;
With long, gloomy stretches of forest,
That lined either bank of the shore.

II

The wind like a spirit of sadness,
Swept mournfully through the tall pines;
While far through the haze of the marshes,
Shone the fires of the enemy's lines.
Now, hushed was the voice of the cannon,
The ear-piercing scream of the shell;
And hushed was the voice of the Minnie,
With its hum of a death ringing knell!

III

The hosts that with death had contended,
Now slept on their arms in repose;
And some dreamed of home and their loved ones,
While others still grappled with foes,
And the pale dead, all silent and stark,
Lay stretched on the blood-trampled sod,

3

With dull staring eyes in the moonlight,
 They seemed to look upward to God!

IV

Thus, by the swamps of Pamunky,
 The picket he paced his slow round,
His eye and his ear on the *qui vive*,
 To challenge each sight and each sound.
No sound met his ear save the bull-frog,
 Or sigh of the wind through the pines;
No sight save the dead in the moonlight,
 Or the fires of the enemy's lines.

V

The picket, with comrades in battle,
 Was thoughtless and daring and wild;
But now with the dead in the midnight,
 His heart it was tender and mild!
When out on a scout with the fellows,
 No heart was as void of all fear;
But now, as he gazed on the vanquished,
 He brushed off the fast falling tear!

VI

As sadly he leaned on his rifle,
 Alone in that field with the slain;
His thoughts travelled home to his loved ones,
 He never might visit again.
And fondly he thought of the sweet one,
 Who hung as a star o'er his life;
And he prayed that the blessing of heaven,
 Might fall on his beautiful wife.

VII

He thought of the dear angel cherubs,
 That now were reposing in sleep,
And he prayed that the Father Eternal!

Their footsteps through life would still keep!
And he thought when this War's fearful havoc,
With all its red carnage would cease;
When the land would arise from her sadness,
And bask in the sunshine of Peace!

VIII

Once more, in his home with his loved ones,
Made dearer by absence and toil;
Surrounded with all those endearments,
So fitted from care to beguile;
He'd sit by the hearth in the winter,
And tell of the dangers when o'er—
But, hark! to the ring of that rifle,
That comes from the far away shore!

IX

O God! that his dream should be broken,
By the hand of a treacherous foe,
O God! that the blood of the valient,
Unavenged is permitted to flow!
Backward he reels; his face to the sky,
He sinks with a groan, to the ground,
While the tide of his young, noble life,
Leaps red from the wide, gaping wound!

X

"My wife—my children—my country—my flag—
God bless and preserve them forever!"
He paused—and under the shadow of Death
He passed with a groan and a shiver!
Rigid and pale, in the sickly moonbeams,
He lay on the blood-clotted sward;
Thus the brave picket reposing was found
By his comrades when changing the guard!

## A REVERY IN WAR TIME.

---

I

I'm weary of the city, with its alleys dark and dun,
Whose haunts are seldom gladdened by the golden summer's sun;
Where flowery scented zophyrs never fan the fevered brain,
Where grinding toil and misery, rack the weary soul with pain!

II

Where no angel smiling flowerets are opening to the view,
As low they bend in beauty, 'neath the morning's pearly dew;
Or hedgrows sweetly laden with the flowery breath of May,
Or song of woodland choristers that hail the blush of day!

III

As it rises o'er the mountains, in gilded glory bright,
And quenches with its ruby smiles those watchmen of the night,
That stood at Heaven's celestial gate throughout the sleeping hours,
To guard their sisters of the earth, the lovely sleeping flowers!

IV

Here, no crystal streamlet gushing, in sighing numbers roll,
In tides of thrilling gladness that o'erpower the human soul;
Here no waving woodlands tempt the thoughtful wanderer's tread,
Nor strain of joyous music from the warbler's overhead!

V

No stern and rugged mountains rise in all their grand array,
That with their stony turrets cleave the glorious vault of day;
Where gathering mists in grandeur swath each mighty giant's form,
The sheath where rests the lighning's brand against the coming storm!

VI

Here, nature has no influence upon the racking strife,
Where crime's dark billow's sweep the shores of this sad City life;
Our forest here is chimney-pots, that rise both dark and grim,
Like swarthy giants frowning in the morning's twilight dim!

VII

And our song bird is the sparrow, from some old smoky tile,
Or song of captive wild bird, with breaking heart the while;
And our crystal brooks the kennel, whose waters seldom run,
With mists of deadly pestilence, drawn from it by the sun!

VIII

Oh! I'm weary of the city with its never-dying hum,
Where the plaint of sin and sorrow, with affliction's never dumb;
Where the grinding din of traffic is ne'er silent in the street,
Whose echoes slumber never with the tread of human feet!

IX

Where human life but vegetates, in cold and cheerless gloom,
And lives in death till death brings life, beyond the voiceless tomb!
'Tis morn upon the mountains, where her beauty bright appears,
But morn within the city wakes its crowds to toil and tears!

X

Within each dark and narrow lane, within each filthy den,
O, what a sea of sorrow lurks, unknown to feeling men;
Of poverty and wretchedness—while, morning, noon, and even,
The gloomy mists of untold crimes rise to avenging Heaven!

II

Upon this troubled sea of life, that surges to and fro,
How many human bubbles glide down to the gulf of woe!
Here, bloated drunkards madly reel—a blur to human name—
Here, flare the painted sisterhood, lost to all sense of shame!

XII.

Thus, the churning waves of sorrow forever round us roll,
Whose dark and poisoned billows break upon the weary soul,
And sucks us, with its hungry lips, into its greedy womb,
Then throws our forms, dismantled wrecks, into the yawning tomb!

XIII

I'm weary of the city, with its misery and its care,
Its cries of bitter anguish, and its faces of despair;
I long to tread the mountain, or the flower-bespangled sod,
To see in Nature's face displayed the boundless love of God!

XIV

See, here, what mean and sordid souls are sheathed within the breast,
With grinding greed and avarice upon the face expressed;
See how they slink with stealty step, along each thoroughfare,
Their pocket's lined with shining gold, wrung from the poor's despair!

XV

They live in sumptuous grandeur—aye, all that earth affords,
Is heaped in shining splendor upon their groaning boards;
Of all that's rare in every land, and every sea they dine;
While crystal goblets brightly flash with ancient ruby wine!

XVI

But not a thought have they to spare, amidst their countless sweets,
For that poor shivering, starving wretch, that's groaning in the streets;
And while their joyous revelry is swelling wild and high,
They leave him in his abject woe, of utter want to die!

XVII

O, I'm weary of the city, with its misery and its art,
Where Truth and Virtue, outcasts all, are driven from the heart;
Where cant and foul hypocrisy are patent everywhere,
And make this world a living hell—that God made bright and fair!

XVIII

And e'en the men ordained by Him to point the Heavenly road,
Where bliss and joy immortal reign, before the throne of God,
With self-complacent air they mount upon their tiny shelves,
And spend their little hour or two to magnify themselves;

XIX

While patriots on every hand desire the state to nurse,
To guide her from destruction's rock, and fill their greedy purse;
Perchance to save, perchance to wreck—no, not a straw they care,
So that their party may have place, and they of spoils a share.

XX

O, give us God! a living bard—a man of mighty soul,
Whose spirit, filled with fire from Thee, may permeate the whole,
Degenerate, selfish sons of men, who live but for their own,
To whom the golden rule of Christ is language all unknown,

XXI

And bid him strike his golden lyre with Heaven-directed hand,
Till once his quivering voice of song shall thrill through every land,
Till every human soul shall melt before its holy fire—
Till fraud and wrong and sin, consumed, shall in its flame expire.

XXII

Methinks me sees the golden age amid the withered years—
The ripe and luscious fruit of Time, which to mine eye appears—
When mankind, like the chrysalis, shall burst his selfish shell,
And to a higher, nobler life exultingly shall swell,

XXIII

And bask forever in the light of God's approving smile,
When Peace and Love and Harmony, shall rule instead of guile;
And like the sons of Noah, seek to hide the shame of wrong,—
To lift the erring and despised to Heaven's exulting throng;

XXIV

When War, with all its horrid feast of carnage and of gore,
Shall be a thrilling memory of the fearful days of yore;
When in the Peace and Light of God, the happy earth shall smile,
And cast her weary load of sin, and rest from all her toil—

XXV

That happy time predicted by the bard of ancient
days,
When all discordant elements shall chant Jehovah's
praise;
When love shall gird the human race with one bright
golden chain,
And sin no longer smear the soul with its grim
hellish stain.

XXVI

But while I mused the spell was broke by war's
discordant cry,
Whose vollied thunders shook the earth and rent the
starry sky;
And through the streets the measured tread of armed
men swept past,
While wild their martial music swelled upon the
wailing blast.

XXVII

And bright the 'broidered banners flashed out on the
golden day,
And loud the shout of thousands rung, all ready for
the fray;
Who freely offered up their lives our heritage to
save,
From the foul pollution of each banded traitor knave;

XXVIII

They came in countless thousands, like the leaves
in Autumn's blast,
And to the burning front of war heroicly they passed
Leaving wives and mothers and still dearer ones in
tears,
To grope in lonely sorrow through the dark of future
years!

XXIX

For the nation cried in anguish of its bitter dark despair,
For the tiger that she nursed had now bounded from its lair;
Despite of love and kindness—aye, all gratitude forgot,
It hung with savage fangs unto its mother's bleeding throat!

XXX

And tried to make a hissing and reproach o'er all the earth,
Of that dear land that nourished it and gave its being birth!
For this our City's echoes are constant ringing out
The ceaseless tread of countless men who peal their battle shout!

XXXI

Oh, God! it is a sick'ning thought that's sweeping through my brain,
How few of all these gallant men shall e're return again,
To cheer the hearts made desolate by war's destroying hand,
That spreads destruction's fearful pall across our noble land.

XXXII

I'm weary of the City, aye, the world, with all its woe,
Whose scalding tears of bitter grief in ceaseless torrents flow;
I long for that auspicious day to dawn upon the heart,
When fraud and wrong and every woe shall from the earth depart!

And though the present hour is dark, and the promise seems to fail,
Yet still I cherish lasting faith, God's word must sure prevail;
When our land from out her baptism, shall come in glory forth,
And be the light of God to all the nations of the earth!

## PRAY FOR FATHER AFAR.

I

O, God! how the wild hurricane rages,
And rattles at every pane,
While it mournfully moans in the chimney,
Like a being in mortal pain.
And the rain in torrents descending,
Beats a tattoo on the shingles,
While the boom of the far-away thunder
In the grand symphony mingles!

II

Hark! how mournful the trees are complaining,
As of their bright plumage they're shorn,
And hear how they are snapping and crashing,
As up by the roots they are torn!
While the stream that runs red from the mountain,
Sweeps past with, a deafening roar,
And the white-lipped waves of the ocean
Break their wrath on the rocky-bound shore!

III

Children, come, gather around by the fire,
While it burns so cozy and bright;
And with reverence we'll thank the Great Father,
For shelter on such a wild night!

And behold, where the light through the casement
  Makes a bright, golden lane through the gloom,
While here we sit snug in the parlor,
  And lists to the dread hurricane's spoom!

IV

But pray, my dear little prattlers, pray
  For father, dear father afar,
Who has gone at the call of his country,
  To th' red burning tempest of war!
And it may be alone as a picket,
  He stands, in the wild, driving rain.
Or it may be—O God! how I tremble—
  He lies 'mongst the mangled and slain.

V

And my heart in its agony sickens,
  While the blood flies up to my brain,
As I think on the form of my darling,
  Lying dead on the wet, trodden plain;
And I stretch out the arms of affection,
  Away, through the fast-driving storm,
Far away, to the red field of slaughter,
  To snatch up his poor mangled form!

VI

There's a weight hangs like lead at my bosom,
  A grief that is gnawing my soul,
A dark premonition of evil,
  That laughs at my feeble control.
Then pray! my dear little prattlers, pray!
  For father, dear father, afar,
That God in compassion would spare him,
  And bring him all safe from the war!

## THE WIFE'S PRAYER.

I

The fire in the grate had smouldered low,
And left but a dull leaden ash;
While the lamp on the mantel burned dim,
With a faint and a flickering flash;
And the sweet little prattlers now lay
In the lap of bright, rosy sleep,—
Heedless of all the wild, raging tempest
And th' vigil their mother did keep.

II

She paced up and down with a nervous tread
In the dusk of her lonely room;
Then pressed her hot brow upon the cold glass,
As she tried to peer through the gloom.
And as she gazed down the midnight's black throat,
All was dismal and rayless, save
The flash of th' rain that fell on the pain,
Or the foam of the breaking wave.

III

She turned away with a heavy heart,
And sunk on the floor by a chair,
And covered her face with her burning palms,
And gave vent to her wild despair.
"Have mercy! have mercy! great God!" she cries,
Through the mist of her blinding tears;
"Have mercy! have mercy, and save my beloved
From the fate which my bosom fears!

IV

"O God! great God! thou fountain of Love!
Thy promise before Thee I plead:
Have mercy, O Lord! on the dust of thy hands,

And crush not a poor bruised reed.
O God! lend an ear to my poor feeble cry,
From the depths of darkness and tears!
Spare us, O Lord, from the stroke of my wrath,
I' the midst of our sorrowful years!

V

"O God! from the dust and ashes of grief
I stretch feeble hands unto Thee,
As a little babe waileth out i' the dark
The face of its mother to see.
Thou hearest the cry of the raven's young
And the roar of the beasts of prey—
Shall the wild heart-wail of thy children, God,
Be still less in thy sight than they?

VI

"O, Omnipotent God, in thy glory
The light as a garment you wear;
Then, oh, leave me not, Father, in blindness,
To grope through the gloom of despair.
Christ, in mercy remember thy sorrow,
With all its great mountain of woes—
The agony and sweat of the garden,
The cross in the midst of thy foes!

VII

"O God! is thine ear closed against mercy?
Are the heavens around Thee as brass,
That the cry of those ready to perish,
No more to thy presence may pass?
Hear me! O, hear, Almighty Jehovah!
I perish, I sink 'neath my load!
Mercy! have mercy, Father Eternal!
Have mercy! have mercy, O God!"

## ANGELS OF MERCY.

TO OUR PATRIOTIC WOMEN.

I

May God's benison rest on you,
Ye bright and noble band,
That like a golden glory shines
Mid the darkness of the land;
Like shining angels through the streets,
From house to house you go,
With gentle hearts and tender hands,
To soothe the pangs of wo.

II

To tend our sick and wounded braves,
Who gallantly went forth,
To battle for the good old cause,
And vindicate the North!
With gentle words and kindly deeds,
You soothe their troubled bed;
While blessings on your noble hearts,
By dying lips are said!

III

While widows and their orphans bless
Your tender-hearted care,
For plucking Famine from their throats,
And from their hearts Despair!
With Christ-like footsteps still ye tread
Life's darkness day by day;
While Mercy, like a line of light,
Still marks your shining way!

IV

It is not in the hurricane
Of war's red flaming breath,

To snatch the conqueror's laurel
  I' the burning throat of Death!
Nor amidst the wild excitement
  Of battle's dire alarms,
Mid the shout of foes contending,
  And th' deaf'ning clash of arms!

V

But on a field unmarked, unknown,
  Your battles all are fought,
And though men seldom ever hear
  The victories ye have wrought;
Yet mid the universe at compt,
  You'll hear the joyful word,
"Well done, my servants, good and true,
  Be joyful with your Lord!"

---

## THE NIGHT AFTER THE BATTLE.

I

The moon through the rack of the driving clouds,
  Like a frightened creature swept,
As if nerved with despair, from crag to crag
  Of the driving scud she lept;
And the pale stars peered through the murky gloom
  At th' flight of their queen so fair;
While some in their terror dropped through the void
  Like red burning bombs in the air.

II

And stern Mars shone forth with his bloodshot eye,
  Through the night's black driving bars,
Presaging to earth and her countless hosts
  Wild tumults and crimson wars,
And the wind with its trembling fingers smote

The leaves from the forest trees,
While it struck the strings of its viewless harp
To wild and weird melodies.

III

But there were sights and sounds more drear by far
Than clouds or piping blast,
For through that field of life, from dawn till dusk,
The grim reaper Death had passed!
His arm might be stiff and his sickle dull,
From his crop of human grain,
For the streams ran red and the meadow groaned
With its weight of ghastly slain!

IV

The rifle and mortar, and Parrot gun
Had belched like the fires of hell,
And th' sickle of Death mowed its living swath
With grape and the bursting shell;
And the charging squadrons thundering dashed
Till they shook the moaning earth,
While heaven in pity vailed her fair face,
And hell shrieked wildly with mirth!

V

Thus from gray-eyed dawn till the dusky eve
The battling hosts contended,
Till night, o'er the scene of carnage and woe,
In dewy tears decended;
When the serried hosts of friend and of foe
Retired from the field of strife,
Leaving at eve ten thousand mangled dead
Who at dawn were full of life,

VI

The while thousands of wounded groaning lay
In their pain and dark despair,

And the wounded coursers plunged 'mid the dead,
While their screams disturbed the air.
"Water, cool water, O give me to drink,
My blood is scorching like fire,
Give me to drink from my own father's well—
Drink—drink—O, God, I expire!"

VII

"Alone! alone! on the red field of fame,
Dear maid, I perish afar,
But still as in life, thou ever hast been,
In death thou art my lode star!
Dear Ella, this picture you gave ere we marched,
Tis dyed with life's crimson gore,
Ella, I kiss thee, 'mid darkness of death—"
He ceased—the brave was no more.

VIII

"Come, give me your hand my own faithful wife,
My fingers are cold and stark,
I feel as my heart were a mountain of ice—
Now fare thee well, all is dark!"
'Twas thus that our wounded and dying braves,
On the field untended lay,
Till the darkness fled and the blushing dawn
Had bloomed to the perfect day!

---

## THE UNION TRIUMPH AT THE POLLS.*

I

Then up, up, hurra!
Let our battle flag wave.
Now we're united,

*This poem was written expressly for the N. Y. Dispatch, and appears by their permission.

The old Union to save,
From foul traitor hands,
Who would dare to pull down,
Our bright starry gem,
Our own flag of renown!

II

That flaunted in pride,
In the face of all foes;
Till once in their hate.
Her own children arose,
And in their fierce madness,
They have sought to deform
Freedom's last refuge
From Tyranny's storm!

III

But up, up, hurra!
For united we stand,
With Freedom's bright glave,
In a firm, steady hand;
Resolved that we'll fight.
Till red treason is hurl'd,
Down, down t' the dust,
In despite of the world.

IV

Hail to the triumph
We have gained at the polls,
Its voice like th' thunder,
All invincibly rolls!
And tells o'er the earth
That we still will uphold.
The Stars and the Stripes
Which our father's unroll'd!

V

Once more Father Abe
  Thy command has gone forth,
And free we obey,
  With the strength of the North;
Whose sons are resolved,
  Let whatever betide,
They'll stand like a rock.
  By the Goverment's side!

---

VI

I hear their might tread,
  As they're marching through the land,
They come in valiant pride,
  A brave heroic band;
Who leave their all behind,
  For wounds and death before,
As did their gallant sires
  In th' glorious days of yore!

VII

From Maine's rude stormy coast,
I hear the battle cry,
"Dirego" shakes the woods, *
  And rends the starry sky;
While from out the forest
  And from the rock-bound shore.
I see a noble host
  In serried columns pour.

VIII

While bright New Hampshire's sun †
  Displays its morning light,

---

* "Dirego,"—I direct—is the motto of Maine.

† The rising sun dispelling the dark clouds of night, is part of the arms of New Hampshire.

Just as her banners shine,
On the nation's dismal night;
The while her noble sons
Are ready for the fray,
Dispelling Treason's gloom,
And restoring Freedom's sway.

IX

And Vermont's motto shines,
Amid the dismal rack,
"Unity and Freedom," *
Reveals her steady track!
Freedom for the bondmen,
And Unity for all;
Thus her gallant heroes
Hath made their battle call.

X

Next, brave Massachusetts,
With her bright, naked blade,
"Peace under Liberty," †
She shouteth, undismayed.
First t' fall at Lexington,
And first at Baltimore—
Sons all worthy of the sires
That fell in days of yore.

XI

Rhode Island with her shield
Of Hope upon the tide, ‡
Hath ranged her little band
On Freedom's bleeding side.

---

* Freedom and Unity is the motto of Vermont.

† "Ense petit placidam sub libertate quietem." By the sword she sheeks peace under liberty, is the motto of Massachusetts.

‡ The arms of Rhode Island is a shield with an anchor, all floating on the sea, while her motto is "Hope."

And brave Connecticut,
  Her motto still her stay;
"He who hath transplanted,
  Will still maintain our sway!"*

XII

Now, see, the Empire State
  Is marching in the van—
"Excelsior," her cry,†
  She peeleth still to man,
While her countless thousands
  Have shed a purple sea
To restore th' stricken land
  To it lost Unity.

XIII

And still they forward march
  At their country's call.
Ever foremost in the strife,
  To leave, the last of all.
And Pennsylvania springs‡
  Upon her wild mustang,
And leading in the charge,
  She seeks the battle's clang!

XIV

The latest born of all
  The noble sisterhood‖
Is foremost in the cause
  To shed her infant blood;
And may sweet Maryland

* "Qui transtulit sustinet." He who transplanted, still sustains, is the motto of Connecticut.

† "Excelsior" Higher. The motto of New York.

‡ The shield of Pennsylvania is supported by two wild horses rampant.

‖ Western Virginia.

"Increase and multiply,"*
Till not a stain of blood
Shall on her fingers lie.

XV

Kentucky has arose.
Obedient to the call,
And on the "bloody ground"†
Hath let her life-blood fall;
While from the crucible
Ohio cometh bright,
And bares her noble arm
In the cause of Truth and Right!

XVI

The while brave Michigan
Hath gave her strength and might,
And still her daring sons
Are ready for the fight.
Next Indiana comes,
With Illinois the brave,
They're marching side by side
The Old Union still to save.

XVII

Missouri in her thrall,
Hath broke the galling chain,
And seeks in liberty
Her birthright to maintain;
Iowa, the valiant,
Is ever in the front,
Nor is Wisconsin far behind
In the battle's brunt.

* "Crestcite et multiplicamini"—increase and multiply. The motto of Maryland.

† "The dark and bloody grounds." The old name of Kentucky.

XVIII

And California
  Keeps steps in this grand march;
While Minnesota stands,
  Like a Keystone in th' arch;
And our noble Kansas,
  Though bleeding at each pore,
With a heart undaunted,
  She seeks the battle's roar!

XIX

And gallant Delaware,
  Despite her rebel swarms,
Hath heard her country's call
  And nobly sprung to arms.
'Tis thus the States are leagued,
  For one grand end sublime,
To leave th' starry circle
  Unbroken to all time!

## THE SOLDIER'S BRIDE.

I

Afar upon the battle-plain,
  The dewy eve descended,
Where brave young Henry dying lay,
  Amid the dead untended.
The pulse of life was ebbing fast,
  His eyes were dim already,
His feeble voice was faint and low,
  His gory hand unsteady!

II

"Oh God!" the dying soldier cried,
  "If she were only here—"

When "Henry! Henry," through the gloom,
  Rang in his dying ear.
Then fondly clasped within her arms,
  She kissed his marble brow,
He only smiled—his spirit passed,
  For death had claimed him now!

III

"Awake! awake! my own beloved!"
  The frantic maiden cried;
Then swooning sunk upon his corse,
  And ere the morn she died!
Now calmly sleeping on that plain,
  They've laid them side by side;
Secure from all the storms of life,
  The soldier and his bride!

## GIVE ME YOUR HAND JOHNNY BULL.

I

Give me your hand Johnny Bull,
  That hand that should ever be mine,
Heed not the fanatical fool,
  His curse, or his foul wolfish whine;
Who seeks to embrue our right hands,
  In the life-blood of each other;
To send the red torch through our lands,
  And hound on brother 'gainst brother!

II

Our language, our literature's one,
  Our creed and our God are the same,
While we are still father and son,
  And all that we differ 's in name,
We honor the stock whence we sprung,

Are proud of the laws of our line;
For us a great Shakspere has sung,
While Franklin and Morse they are thine!

III

Our freedom but differs in name,
The first of its kind upon earth;—
We never will put you to shame,
For giving our nation its birth;
But let us forget all the spleen,
And rancor of old family jars;
And let the red cross in its sheen,
Fly intwined with the stripes and the stars!

IV

Then give me your hand Johnny Bull,
That hand that's ne'er gave to a lie;
And woe to the knave or his tool,
That comes between Johnny and I,
Back to back, 'gainst the world we'll stand,
Sublime in the faith of the past;
With Freedom's red glave in our hand,
We'll prove true to that faith to th' last.

---

## TELL ME OF MY BOY.

---

I

O tell me of my boy,
My boy so good and brave;
Who at his country's call,
Went forth its flag to save.
O tell me of his deeds,
On Antietam's day,
When like a hero bold,
He sought the thickest fray.

II

O read from that old Times,—
  My sight is growing dim,—
And let me hear the words,
  His Colonel said of him,—
I know them all by heart,
  For in the peaceful night,
When the house is calm and still,
  I say them till 'tis light!

III

How "in that fearful hour,
  When his Division broke,
And reeled beneath the weight,
  Of that wild battle shock;
He boldly sprung in front,
  And waved his blood-red brand,
And shouted "comrades brave,
  Who'll die for our dear land;"

IV

They rallied at his word,
  And dashed upon the foe,
Dealing death and wounds,
  In every fearful blow,
A minute hand to hand,
  Their gleaming bayonets clashed,
But like a wintery flood,
  Our heroes boldly dashed;

V

Upon the foemen's lines,
  Till they waver and they reel,
Beneath our steady fire,
  And the pressure of our steel!
But in that glorious hour,

When "Victory" rent the air,
A Rebel bullet smote,
Our brave Lieutenant Clair!

VI

He never breathed nor spoke,
But sunk upon the sod,
While his proud spirit passed,
Into the arms of God!
A nobler youth than he,
Or one more true, or brave,
Ne'er breathed upon the earth,
Or filled a soldier's grave!

VII

You see the tears are falling,
Adown my aged cheek,
But Oh! it cheers my heart,
To hear my neighbors speak
Of that dear boy of mine,
Who perished on that day,
In doing daring deeds,
That won us Victory!

VIII

Nor would I give my boy,
Though dead and in the clay,
For any living son,
That walks the earth to day!
So tell me of my boy,
My boy so good and brave,
Who at his country's call,
Went forth its flag to save!

## FORT SUMPTER.

I

Hark! brothers, hark, 'to the distant din,
That breaks through the startled night,
To the bugle's blare and the red fire's glare
That tell of the distant fight;
Where the perjured traitor's gathering host
Encircle a valiant band;
Who proudly dare, in the face of despair,
To die for the glorious land!

II

A hundred noble hearts are there,
With a leader tried and true';
While flaunting there, in the southern air,
Is the glorious red white and blue!
They have eat th' last meal from their famished
store,
While the shot fell hot and fast;
And now in the might, of God and the right;
They answer the foe at last!

III

Their shot and their shell, like the bolts of hell,
Scatter death 'mid the traitor host;
And a hundred fell, while their funeral knell,
Was the boom from the 'leagured post!
And thus for two days 'mid fire and smoke,
Those gallant heroes fought;
While their shot and their shell, like the bolts of
hell,
A thousand foeman smote!

IV

Till the red shot by the foemen fired,

Had lit Fort Sumpter's tower's;
Till the fire demon with his red arms,
Had swathed that band of ours;
Still in the heat of the scorching flames,
Our banner proudly floats,
While the red tempest of wounds and death,
Is poured from our cannon's throats."

V

At length to hunger and toil they yield,—
So the Traitors need not boast,
For that valiant band, could still withstand,
The might of the Rebel host!
But hunger and toil, and schorching fire,
And not the battle's blast;
Bid their brave leader yield the Fort,
To their Country's foes at last!

## LULABY.

I

Lulaby, lulaby,
O hush my dear babe,
On mother's warm bosom,
Thy red cheek is laid;
While she thinks of father,
Who slumbers to-night,
All mangled and cold,
On th' red field of fight!

II

Lulaby, lulaby,
O creep to my breast,
And with thy soft cooing,
Sing thee to rest;

While your poor mother's thoughts,
Must stray through the gloom,
Thus to weep in the dark,
O'er that bloody tomb!

III

Lulaby, lulaby,
You have nought to fear,
For though the storm rages,
Your mother is near;
While her lone window's tears,
Are wetting her pillow,
For father that's sleeping,
Beneath the marsh willow!

IV

Lulaby, lulaby,
Creep close to my heart,
For since father was slain,
Thrice dearer thou art!
But now my sweet orphan,
Is sleeping so still,
I'll ease my poor heart,
By weeping my fill!

---

## MARCH ON YE GALLANT BRAVES!

---

I

March on, ye gallant braves,
Upon the path of glory,
Fear not the Traitor knaves,
In darkest crimes grown hoary;
Long have they ruled in blood,
In fiendish wrath and glee-man,
But little understood the
The metal of the free-man!

II

They thought by crack of whip,
  To make us shake and shiver,
And in their greedy grip,
  To make us slave for-ever;
But now the giant North,
  Has woke up from her dreaming,
And goes to battle forth,
  With star-gemm'd banner streaming.

III

Still streaming as of yore,
  When we met the proud enslaver,
And made him quell before
  Our country's first endeavor!
Then march, ye gallant band
  To triumph and to glory,
The prais'd of every land,
  The bravest sons of story!

---

## AROUSE!

I

Arouse! brothers, 'rouse!
  For our dear native land;
And strike for its glory
  With heart and with hand!
While round the old banner
  We will rally in pride,
And scatter the Traitors,
  Would dare to deride!

II

Or spurn the bright stars,
  Which our fathers unfurled,
The hope of the earth

And the light of the world!
Arouse! brothers, 'rouse!
For our dear native land!
And strike for its honor,
With heart and with hand!

---

## SONG OF THE EXEMPTS.

---

I

I'm exempt, I'm exempt, I vow and declare,
I'm exempt, I'm exempt from the "draft" I will swear,
What, though the rebels our soil may invade,
And wipe out each general of pick-axe and spade?
Oh! what do I care though a million are slain;
And our starry-gemmed banner is tramped on the plain?
Oh! what do I care, who may fail or may thrive,
I'm exempt, I'm exempt, I'm o'er forty-five!

II

I'm exempt, I'm exempt, I vow and declare,
I'm exempt, I'm exempt from the "draft" I will swear,
Oh! what do I care, what my neighbors may say,
That I've jumped o'er ten years in less than a day?
Oh! what do I care for my nation and laws?
I heed not her shame, I seek not applause;
But still for the *Almighty Dollar* I'll drive,
I'm exempt, I'm exempt, I'm over forty-five!

III

I'm exempt, I'm exempt, I vow and declare,
I'm exempt, I'm exempt from the "draft" I will swear.

I always was healthy from heel unto nobe,
But now I have troubles as many as Job;
You may wink and may sneer, and say "it's all gas,"
That such a lame "*ho'se*" with the doctors won't pass:
But I'm aches, I'm pains, from the head to the toe,
I'm exempt, I'm exempt, from the "draft" you must know!

IV

I'm exempt, I'm exempt, I vow and declare,
I'm exempt, I'm exempt from the "draft" I will swear.
I'm free to confess that I find greater charms,
In a trip to the Province, than taking up arms;
I'm off, I'm off, with the very first train,
And when the war is over I'll come back again:
You call me a sneak—I heed not your twaddle.
I'm exempt, I'm exempt, I mean to *skedaddle!*

---

## A SONG AND A CHEER.

I

A song and a cheer
To the new-born year
As he comes through the midnight down,
We'll bid him God speed,
And pray that his meed
May have Peace and Love for its crown.

II

Then wake, brothers, wake,
And for Love's sweet sake
Let the heavenly stranger in;
To rule and to reign,

And remove each stain
Of hatred, of wrath, and of sin!

III

To blot out the wrong
That has severed so long,
Between man and his brother man,
To banish the strife,
And the jars of life,
That have been humanity's ban!

IV

To quench the wild fire
Of tyranny's ire,
That has deluged the earth with gore,
And break the red brand
In the despot's hand,
And the reign of King Love restore!

V

To heal up the scars
And fratricide wars
Inflicted by men on each other,
To crush out the wrong
Of the weak by the strong—
*Of Cain still slaying his brother.*

VI

Then let hand strike hand
Through our stricken land,
And each heart meet each heart in love,
And with song and with cheer
We'll hail the New Year,
An Angel of Peace from above!

## WAITING.

I

The ruby Sun has sunk
 Like a jewel in the sea,
While twilight softly comes
 In her calm serenity;
Thus leading up Old Night
 Like a pilgrim, by the hand,
In her black-purple robe,
 Starry-gemmed, superbly grand!

II

While silently I sit,
 All alone within my room,
To watch the silver lights,
 As they blossom in the gloom;
And list the night wind's sigh
 As it smites the Autumn leaves,
That fall in blood-red clouds
 Down upon the yellow sheaves!

III

The while hot scalding tears,
 Are swift welling from mine eyes,
To think of that red-field
 Where my mangled lover lies!
Where in youth and beauty,
 And his undaunted might,
He met the Rebel horde,
 In the stormy field of fight.

IV

While the crimson carnage
  Was sweeping to and fro,
He bore his country's flag,
  'Mid the thickest of the foe!
But that deed of daring
  Cost my noble love his life,
And he fell a mangled corse,
  On that bloody field of strife.

V

And now I'm left in tears,
  In my maiden-widowhood,
To mourn my soldier love
  In this lone solitude!
For on that day we wed,
  He went forth with his corps,—
I blessed him as he passed,
  To return to me no more!

VI

My head went swimming round,
  As their platoons marched past,
And my spirit whispered,
  "Look upon him for the last!"
The grief-mist swam before me,
  And my heart felt like a stone;
For, 'mid the cheer of thousands,
  I felt desolate and lone.

VII

Sometimes when I'm musing,
  I leap up from my chair,
For I hear the footstep

Of my darling on the stair;
And I bid him welcome,
But my eyes flood up with tears,
For I'll ne'er behold him,
In the long, long flight of years!

VIII

That stretches dark and dim,
On life's sad dreary road;
Till I shall embrace him,
In the Royal home of God!
Thus I bear my burthen,
Through this long, long dreary way,
Waiting for the promise
Of the Lord's appointed day!

---

## THE NAMELESS BRAVE.

I

In the world's wild strife and conflic,
On life's deadly battle plain,
Where oppression, hate and sorrow,
Count their thousand thousands slain,
In this strife how many heroes
Fall unblazoned by fame,
In the ranks they fought and perished,
Filling graves without a name.

II

Not 'mid carnage did these heroes
Seek the soldiers gorey wreath,
Not by smiting human cattle,

Down upon the field of death,
Nor the trenches' crimson channels,
Nor the daring escalade
Hewing pathways up to glory,
With a keen and gleaming blade.

III

Filling hearts and homes with sadness,
Staining earth with human gore,
Blighting hopes that early perish,
In that sad word "Never-more"
Leaving widows sadly wailing,
For their loved, their precious dead;
With the voice of Rachel crying,
Never to be comforted.

IV

But these heroes, men and women,
In the peaceful walks of life,
Did their noble deeds of daring,
Far from turmoil and from strife,
By the sick-bed and the erring,
Where their words of comfort fall;
By their deeds of gentle mercy,
Like God's blessings, blessing all.

V

By the triumph of their passions,
By their battles in the Right,
By their succor of the helpless,
Of the Right against the Might,
What although they pass unheeded,
O'er life's dark and dreary way,
Though no shouting thousands greet them,
With the crown of Victory?

VI

What, although they are forgotten,
By the Ages as they roll,
Though their names may ne'er be blazoned,
On Fame's bright triumphal scroll?
Yet their deeds shall live forever,
In the record up above,
And their names shall ring with blessings,
From the lips of boundless Love.

---

## PERSEVERE.

I

Art thou one that's meek and lowly,
Striving with the ills of life?
If thy cause be just and holy,
Fear not then to meet the strife:
For thy Maker and thy Father
Soon shall light the darkness drear
Which around thy path may gather—
Courage, then, and persevere!

II

Art thou one who battles bravely
In the cause of truth and right?
Fear not though the arm of knavery
Smite thee in its hour of might—
Still undaunted, boldly forward,
For thy heart has nought to fear;
Still through life be this thy watch-word,
In the truth we'll persevere!

III

For man's mind is of that fashion
That can conquer at its will,
All the evils of each passion,
All that bears the name of ill!
Statesman, poet, father, mother,
Or whatever name you bear;
Turn my erring sister, brother,
Seek the right and persevere!

---

## GIVE US PEACE.

---

I

Give us Peace!
A righteous Peace, O Lord!
Acording to thy word
Let havoc cease!

II

Look on our land,
Our poor afflicted clime,
Thus suffering for our crime
At Thy right hand!

III

O spare us God!
In our Gethsemane,
We look alone to Thee
Who holds the rod!

IV

O not in wrath,
  O not in anger smite!
Yet, lead us into light,
  E'en though by Death!

V

Let havoc cease,
  For as the hungry brood,
Wide gapeth for their food,
  We seek for Peace!

---

## TO THE 79th. N. Y. HIGHLANDERS.

RESPECTFULLY INSCRIBED TO COLONEL MORRISON.

I

Then up, hurra! for the sons of the mountain,
  With their bright tartans and bonnets o' blue,
Fierce as the waves of their own native fountains;
  Brave hearts of steel that are loyal and true,
Sons of the sires, who are famous in story,
  Land of the Bruce, and Wallace, the brave,
March on to triumph, to honor and glory,
  The stars and the stripes from pollution to save.

II

How oft has your slogan rung o'er the battle,
  Telling of death to the treacherous foe,
Yet steady and cool mid musketry's rattle,
  And booming of guns right onward you go.

Then up, hurra! for the sons of the mountain,
  With their bright tartans and bonnets o' blue,
Fierce as the waves of their own native fountains,
  Brave hearts of steel that are loyal and true.

III

A hundred red fields your valor has spoken,
  Worthy the land of the mountain and flood,
Where your thinned ranks, undaunted, unbroken,
  Fought for the Union 'mid carnage and blood,
Then up, hurra! for the sons of the mountain,
  With their bright tartans and bonnets o' blue,
Fierce as the waves of their own native fountains,
  Brave hearts of steel that are loyal and true.

IV

Then hip, hip, hurra! for the land whence they sprung,
  And a cheer for the deeds of their daring,—
Their praise shall be told and their fame shall be sung,—
  In the hour of the nation's despairing!
Then up, hurra! for the sons of the mountain,
  With their bright tartans and bonnets o' blue,
Fierce as the waves of their own native fountains,
  Brave hearts of steel that are loyal and true.

THE

# LILY OF THE WOODS:

## A TALE

OF THE

## MINNESOTA MASSACRE,

BY W. A. DEVON,

Author of "Red-Mark," "Harold," "War Lyrics," etc.

---

We intend to publish the above story, about the end of January. It is said, by those who have read the manuscript, to be one of the most startling and thrilling Tales of Border Life; which has ever been issued from the New York press. The tens of thousands who read the Author's former story of Red Mark will watch with deep anxiety for the appearance of his forthcoming work. The incidents of this powerful narrative, are still fresh in the minds of the people. The wholesale and indiscriminate massacre of men, women, and children, sent a thrill of horror through the great heart of humanity! And our Author with a graphic pen, has portrayed the fearful deeds of cruelty, inflicted by the remorseless savages! and leads the reader on with breathless interest to the last page; every one of which, teems with interest and wild adventure.

The characters are drawn with a master hand. The gentle, loving, Amy Marsden; with all her trials, sufferings and steady constancy to her early love; inspires us with admiration. While the wily hypocrite, the Rev. Paul Knacker, with all his scheming and duplicity, is beautifully portrayed. The brave, but eccentric Bill Ralston, Wolftrap, Joe Painter, and the little Cockney, Dicky Pudding, Esq. "von of the Haristockricy," can not fail to interest and amuse the reader.

While the self-sacrificing and heroic Indian Chief, War Eagle, is without a parallel out of the great works of Cooper.

The plot is well conceived, and excellently carried out; taking the reader altogether by surprise. We are confident that "The Lily of the Woods," will create a greater sensation amongst the reading public than that produced by "Red Mark!"

THE PUBLISHER.

# FREEDOM.

## A Choice Collection:

INSPIRED BY THE

## INCIDENTS AND SCENES OF THE PRESENT WAR

J. F. FEEKS, PUBLISHER,

No. 26 ANN STREET, N. Y.

# FREEDOM.

## A Choice Collection:

INSPIRED BY THE

## INCIDENTS AND SCENES OF THE PRESENT WAR

---

J. F. FEEKS, PUBLISHER,

No. 26 ANN STREET, N. Y.

# CONTENTS.

# SONGS AND BALLADS

OF

# FREEDOM.

## THE AMERICAN FLAG.

The flag of my country! how proudly I hail
Its stripes and its stars, as it floats in the gale;
From battlement, tower and mast, o'er a land
As free as the air by which it is fanned.
A terror alike to the tyrant and slave,
But the standard where rally the good and the brave.

The land it floats o'er is a beautiful land,
They who flung it aloft were a glorious band;
But to guard it from insult and foemen, think you,
There are spirits less daring or hearts now less true?
Be assured in the onset no freeman will lag,
When called to defend the American flag.

His flag is his altar—each hearth is a throno,
The cause of his country he feels as his own,
And proclaims to all tyrants and pitiful elves,
That intelligent freemen can govern themselves.
Be assured that never a freeman will lag,
When called to protect the American flag.

CHORUS—Be assured that never a freeman will lag,
When called to protect the American flag.

## WHO WILL CARE FOR MOTHER NOW?

[Words by Chas. Carroll Sawyer—Music by Chas. F. Thompson. The Music to be had of SAWYER & THOMPSON, 59 Fulton Avenue, Brooklyn, N. Y.]

Why am I so weak and weary?
See how faint my heated breath—
All around to me seems darkness—
Tell me, comrades, is this death?
Ah! how well I know your answer—
To my fate I meekly bow—
If you'll only tell me truly:
Who will care for mother now?

Chorus—Soon with angels I'll be marching,
With bright laurels on my brow—
I have for my Country fallen,
Who will care for mother now?

Who will comfort her in sorrow?
Who will dry the falling tear,
Gently smooth her wrinkled forehead?
Who will whisper words of cheer?
Even now I think I see—her
Kneeling, praying for me! how
Can I leave her in her anguish?
Who will care for mother now? Chorus.

Let this knapsack be my pillow,
And my mantle be the sky;
Hasten, comrades, to the battle!
I will like a soldier die—
Soon with angels I'll be marching,
With bright laurels on my brow;
I have for my Country fallen,
Who will care for mother now? Chorus.

## THE BEAUTIES OF CONSCRIPTION.

BY JEAN VALJEAN.

And thus the "people's sovereignty,"
  Before a despot humbled,
Lies in the dust, 'neath power unjust,
  Its crown and sceptre crumbled—
Their brows distained—like felons chained
  To negroes, called "their betters;"
Their whinings drowned in "*Old John Brown*,"
  Poor "*sovereigns*," wearing fetters!
    Hurrah for the Conscription!
    American Conscription!
Well have they quaffed old Lincoln's Draft.
    Hurrah for the Conscription!

Some think this hideous spectacle
  Should move the heart to sadness,
That fetters ought—O! silly thought—
  Sting freemen's souls to madness!
When has the stock of Plymouth Rock
  Been melted to compunction?
As for Provo's, the wide world knows
  That chaining is their function!
    Hurrah for the Conscription!
    American Conscription!
And for the stock of Plymouth Rock,
    Whence sprung this new Conscription!

What matter if you're "*sandwiched*" in
  A host of sable fellows,
Well flavored men—your kith and kin—
  So Abe and Sumner tell us.
Is not this war, *this murder* for
  The negro—*nolens volens?*

For every three, now killed of ye,
There's just a negro stolen!
And then ye have Conscription,
American Conscription!
Your blood must flow for them ye know.
Hurrah for the Conscription!

---

## SHE'S BLACK, BUT THAT'S NO MATTER.

My Dinah dear, she's as beautiful quite
As a star that shines calmly at the close of the night;
A voice like a siren, a foot like a fay—
"She's just such a gal you don't meet every day!"
(*Spoken.*)—But she's black!
CHORUS—I know she is, but what of that?
You'd love, could you look at her;
I'd have her just the way she is—
She's black, but that's no matter.

She lives on the banks of a bright-flowing stream,
In a cabin that might have been built in a dream,
Surrounded by roses, and woodbines, and leaves,
"That twine and climb up to the eaves."
(*Spoken.*)—But she's so very black;
I know she is, etc.

If ever I marry this dark-colored maid,
You'll believe in the truth of what I have said;
I love her because her complexion will keep,
"And they say that all beauty is only skin-deep."
(*Spoken.*)—But she's black!
I know she is, etc.

## WE COME TO RAISE OUR BANNER.

AIR—"*The Old Granite State.*"

We are Freedom's sons and daughters
  Who love our native land,
We are Freedom's sons and daughters,
  Who love our native land;
And to guard each hill and valley,
And to guard each hill and valley,
  We pledge our heart and hand.

CHORUS—Then high we raise our banner,
  Yes, on high we raise our banner,
  Yes, on high we raise our banner,
    With the stars and stripes so grand,
  And to guard each hill and valley,
  And to guard each hill and valley,
    We pledge our heart and hand.

We never can be conquered,
  Though foes around us rave,
We never can be conquered,
  Though foes around us rave,
For we have right gallant leaders,
For we have right gallant leaders,
  Whose hearts are true and brave.

CHORUS—Then high we raise our banner,
  Yes, on high we raise our banner,
  Yes, on high we raise our banner,
    With the stars and stripes so grand,
  And their shouts to Heaven going, &c.

## I WISH I HAD A FAT CONTRACT.

Sung by Dan Holt, Ethiopian Comedian.

Air—" *Barbara Allan.*"

O white folks! here I is again,
  Where merry hours we passes;
To come out here and see you all,
  I 've left my gin-and-'lasses!
Oh, I 've got my old banjo—
  We know there's music in it;
And I have got a little song,
  And now I'm goin' to sing it.
Chorus: Den I wish I had a fat contract,
    But it ain't no use a-wishin'—
  For I ain't a-goin' to get it,
    'Kase I ain't a politician.

But if I had a fat contract
  To make clothes for de sogers,
De army coats and striped pants,
  It 's den I 'd feel melogious.
I wouldn't use no shoddy,
  Nor no oder stuff dat's rotten;
But I'd use de very best of cloth,
  Widout a bit of cotton.
    Den I wish I had, etc.

Oh, if I had a fat contract
  To make de army shoeses,
I wouldn't do as some folks do,
  Who de so-gi-ers abuses:
I'd make de shoes so tight and strong,
  I'd make them neat and taper,
I'd make them all of leather,
  And I wouldn't use no paper.
    Den I wish I had, etc.

Oh, if I had a fat contract
  To find de pans and kittles,
De blankets, and de oder tings,
  Likewise de sogers' wittles,
I wouldn't give them rotten pork—
  A very nasty trick dat—
Wid salt beef made of leather,
  And de biscuit like a brickbat!
    Den I wish I had, etc.

Oh, if I had a fat contract
  To put down dis rebellion,
I wouldn't do as some folks do,
  Wid cash my pocket swellin':
I'd give de sogers de best of grub,
  And den no foes could bang 'em;
For Davis and his rebel crowd
  I'd furnish rope to hang 'em.
    Den I wish I had, etc.

---

## OUR NEW BATTLE CRY.

Rally, white men, promptly rally,
  Rouse your souls to martial ire;
Man the fort and man the galley,
  Carry southward sword and fire.
Keep your chains as bright as others
While you rivet on your brother's;
  Mount the conqueror's gory car;
    Ride to battle for the nigger,
    Fight the fight out for the nigger,
    Give your hardy limbs and vigor
  To the labor of the war.

Let the share rust in the furrow,
  Gore the soil with shot and shell;
Ply the torch in town and borough,
  Where your fancied foemen dwell.
Whet the sickle to a sabre,
Rob the farmer of his labor,
  Grain fields can't your march debar.
      Forward for the shackled nigger—
      Onward for the grateful nigger,
      Heed not scoffer or intriguer,
  'Tis the watchword of the war.

Heed not warning hands uplifted,
  Nor the tears that orphans shed;
Ask not where the cause has drifted
  For which heroes *might* have bled.
Lend a hand to rivet faster
Chains on freemen—bring disaster
  On the soil whose sons you are.
      Scourge the white man for the nigger;
      Scourge a nation for the nigger,
      To ruin not to right it eager
  With the poisoned scourge of war.

And when the strife is over,
  The battle fought and won,
And when the strife is over,
  The battle fought and won,
We will shout the notes of gladness,
We will shout the notes of gladness,
  In Freedom's happy land.
CHORUS—And high shall wave our banner,
    Yes, on high shall wave our banner,
    Yes, on high shall wave our banner
      With the stars and stripes so grand.
    We will shout the notes of gladness, &c.

## LET ME KISS HIM FOR HIS MOTHER.

Let me kiss him for his Mother,
  Let me kiss his dear youthful brow;
I will love him for his Mother,
  And seek her blessing now.
Kind friends have sooth'd his pillow,
  Have watched his ev'ry care;
Beneath the weeping willow,
  Oh! lay him gently there.
    CHORUS: Sleep, dearest, sleep;
        I love you as a brother;
      Kind friends around you weep,
        I've kissed you for your Mother.

Let me kiss him for his Mother,
  What though left a lone stranger here;
She has loved him as none other,
  I feel her blessing near.
Though cold that form lies sleeping,
  Sweet angels watch around;
Dear friends are near thee weeping;
  Oh! lay him gently down. CHORUS.

Let me kiss him for his Mother,
  Or perchance a fond sister dear;
If a father or a brother,
  I know their blessing's here.
Then kiss him for his Mother:
  'Twill soothe her after-years;
    Farewell, dear stranger, brother,
  Our REQUIEM, our tears! CHORUS.

## KISS ME GOOD NIGHT, MOTHER.

AIR—"*Rock me to Sleep, Mother.*"

All lonely and weary I pace the wet ground,
While evening her curtain is closing around,
The sorrowful night bird is singing her lay,
The welcome of darkness, the dirge of the day,
The voices of daylight have sunken to sleep,
And left me to silence all death-like and deep.
But I may not sleep, for the foe is in sight,
Then kiss me good night, mother—kiss me good night.

I've felt on my cheek the dread rifle-ball's breath;
While comrades around me were falling in death;
I know 'twas thy prayer thro' carnage and strife,
That shielded from Heaven thy soldier-boy's life.
Oh! oft have I wished for thee, mother and home,
When darkness above me was settling in gloom;
But why am I sad, who was wont to be light?
Oh! kiss me good night, mother—kiss me good night.

The sullen foe's watch-fires gleam wide on the hills,
But what is this coldness my bosom that thrills?
And why do I see all the past that is gone?
O Death! hast thou come for me weary, alone?
But hold! I must banish this sadness away;
My watch is near ended; 'tis dawning of day.
That flash—I am shot—the earth fades from my sight—
Quick, kiss me good night, mother—kiss me good night.

Thy spirit, dear mother, presides o'er my sleep,
Thy love and thy care seem my footsteps to keep;
Oh well I remember each word that you said,
Thy last warm fond kiss from my lip has not fled.
Oh be with me, mother, when life is just past,
When the shadow of earth from my eye's fading fast,
And the first glimpse of heaven dawns clear on my sight,
Then kiss me good night, mother—kiss me good night.

Then weep not, dear mother, for death is but sleep,
But longer and sweeter, more calm and more deep;
The spirit away from its prison is borne,
And wakes to the light of a heavenly morn,
When weary and tired of this life it finds rest,
Oh call it not back from the home of the blest.
Remember, dear mother, when death wins the fight,
'Twill not be for long that you kiss me good night.

---

## THREE HUNDRED THOUSAND MORE.

[Music can be had of J. P. Shaw, Publisher, Rochester, N. Y.]

We are coming, Father Abram, three hundred thousand more,
From Mississippi's winding stream, and from New England's shore;
We leave our plows and workshops, our wives and children dear,
With hearts too full for utterance, but with a silent tear.

CHORUS:

We dare not look behind us but steadfastly before,
We are coming, Father Abram, three hundred thousand more.

## WHEN JOHNNY COMES MARCHING HOME.

When Johnny comes marching home again, hurrah hurrah!
We'll give him a hearty welcome then, hurrah, hurrah!
The men will cheer, the boys will shout;
The ladies, they will all turn out,
And we 'll all feel gay,
When Johnny comes marching home.

The old church-bell will peal with joy, hurrah, hurrah!
To welcome home our darling boy, hurrah, hurrah!
The village lads and lasses say
With roses they will strew the way;
And we 'll all feel gay,
When Johnny comes marching home.

Get ready for the Jubilee, hurrah, hurrah!
We 'll give the hero three times three, hurrah, hurrah!
The laurel-wreath is ready now
To place upon his loyal brow;
And we 'll all feel gay,
When Johnny comes marching home.

Let love and friendship on that day, hurrah, hurrah!
Their choicest treasures then display, hurrah, hurrah!
And let each one perform some part
To fill with joy the warrior's heart;
And we'll all feel gay.
When Johnny comes marching home.

## BLOW YOUR HORN, GABRIEL.

**Ethiopian Song and Dance.**

AIR—" *Going round the Horn.*"

I've got a song to sing to you, so list to what I say—
About de Nigger Destiny I'll tell you right away:
"De Union!" used to be de cry—for dat we went it strong;
But now de motto seems to be, "De niggër, right or wrong!"

CHORUS.

Oh, de moke! oh, de moke! oh, de moke!
Oh, oh, oh! ho, ho!

Blow your horn, Gabriel, and sound it frough de land,
For de niggers now have got a jubilee;
Meet me in de White House, I'll take you by de hand,
For de darkey am de ruler ob de day!

Now in de house of Congress a speech is never spoke
Widout dey have de nigger in—dey're bound to please de moke;
But what dey're gwine to do wid him I'd really like to know:
I'ts very well to set him free—but where's he gwan to go?

Oh, de moke, etc.

Some speak of colonizin' de niggers—dey would make
A colored Mormon settlement, like Brigham's at Salt Lake;

And some 'd make dem sogers—dis darkey wouldn't keer,
If dey'd only make him general, a bully brigadier!
Oh, de moke, etc.

To run de mokes for office, wid some it is de plan;
Dey say de nigger's just as good as "any oder man."
But one ting I can tell—when all de fuss is o'er,
De nig'll be no better off dan what he was before!
Oh, de moke, etc.

---

## BATTLE OF LEXINGTON.

Slowly the mist o'er the meadow was creeping,
Bright on the dewy buds glistened the sun,
When from his couch—while his children were sleeping,
Rose the bold patriot and shouldered his gun.
Waving her golden vail,
Over the silent dale,
Blithe looked the morning on cottage and spire;
Hushed was his parting sigh,
While from his noble eye,
Flashed the last sparkle of liberty's fire.

Snow girdled crags, where the hoarse wind is raving
Rocks where the weary floods murmur and wail;
Wilds where the fern by the furrow is waving,
Reeled with the echoes that rode on the gale.
Far as the tempest thrills,
Over the darkened hills,
Far as the sunshine streams over the plain,
Roused by the tyrant band,
Woke all the mighty land,
Girded for battle from mountain and main.

Green be the graves where her martyrs are lying!
Shroudless and tombless they sunk to their rest,
While o'er their ashes the starry flag flying,
Soars the proud eagle they roused from his rest.
Borne on her northern pine,
Long o'er the foaming brine,
Spread her broad banner to storm and to sun;
Heaven keep her ever free,
Wide as her land and sea,
Floats the fair emblem her heroes have won.

---

## HOW ARE YOU, SHODDY?

Oh! a wonderful man is a shoddy contractor,
A man very useful, indeed—to himself.
The purest of patriots is he in fact, or
Enough so to gain him a plenty of pelf.
While our soldiers are cold on the battlefield lying,
Or shedding their blood for the Union, still
He is aiding the cause of the Union by trying
His pockets, by contracts for shoddy, to fill.

CHORUS:

Shod-shod-shoddy! How are you, Shoddy?
There 's a place that is made for the meanest of men,
And a great day of judgment that's certainly coming,
And where, Mr. Shoddy, will you be then?

But freely his errors should all be forgiven,
When his pockets so nicely are lined with the tin;
His money should buy him a ticket to heaven,
For surely so rich a man never can sin.

His wife, who a short time ago was plain Bridget,
As Mrs. Fitz-Shoddy she now feels her oats;
She can ride, she can dress, she can primp and can fidget,
For her husband is able to pay all her notes.
CHORUS—Shod-shod-shoddy! &c.

While others are pouring their blood and their treasure
For Union and Liberty, freely and well,
Our Mr. Fitz-Shoddy is taking his pleasure,
Or seeking his rotten old shoddy to sell.
In his ill-gotten gains for a while he may revel,
Secure from all punishment, heedless of blame,
But his soul has been bartered away to the devil,
And soon the Old Nick will his property claim.
CHORUS—Shod-shod-shoddy! &c.

---

## CABINET PICTURES.

TUNE—"*Hurrah for the bonnets o' blue.*"

There was an Attorney named Lincoln,
The last for a statesman you'd think on;
All danger was smoke,
If he had but his joke,
And could browse, and tell stories, and wink on.

There was an old pilot named Seward,
Who never believed that it blew hard;
So he woke up too late,
When the ship of the state
Was drifting on sand banks to leeward.

There was a purse-bearer named Chase,
Who made paper and gold run a race,
And invented the green-back
That was ne'er to be seen back
At the customs—a very hard case.

There was an old fogie named Welles,
Quite worthy of cap and of bells,
For he thought that a pirate,
Who steamed at a great rate,
Would wait to be riddled with shells.

There was an attorney named Bates,
Chief adviser at law for the States;
But as never a word
Of his pleading is heard,
Who can possibly tell how he rates?

There was an old post-man named Blair,
Disposed to do something quite fair,
But fanatical fury
Made Blair of Missouri,
In the pranks of the cabinet share.

There was an old war-ass named Stanton,
Almost an American Danton,
Though he thinks he's designed
To astonish mankind
Round the world from Chicago to Canton.

There was an old poet named Bryant,
On Parnassus by no means a giant,
Yet he scowls like a ghost,
As he doles from a *Post*
His humanities grim and defiant.

There was a queer parson named Beecher,
Not of Christ, but of bloodshed, a teacher;
    It was always a trifle
    Whether—Bible or rifle,
Wrought the aim of this blasphemous preacher.

---

## OLD SHODDY.

TUNE—"*The Friar of Orders Gray.*"

Old Shoddy sits in his easy chair,
  And cracks his jokes and drinks his ale,
Dumb to the shivering soldier's prayer,
  Deaf to the widows' and orphans' wail.
His coat is as warm as the fleece unshorn;
  Of a "golden fleece" he is dreaming still;
And the music that lulls him night and morn,
  Is the hum-hum-hum of the shoddy mill.

Clashing cylinders, whizzing wheels,
  Rend and ravel and tear and pick;
What can resist the hooks of steel,
  Sharp as the claws of the ancient Nick?
Cast-off mantle of millionaire,
  Pestilent vagrant's vesture chill,
Rags of miser or beggar bare,
  *All* are "grist" for the shoddy mill.

Worthless waste and worn-out wool,
  Flung together a specious *sham!*
With just enough of the "fleece" to pull
  Over the eyes of Uncle Sam.

Cunningly twisted through web and woof,
  Not "shirt of Nesus" such power to kill;
Look how the prints of his hideous hoof
  Track the fiend of the shoddy mill.

A soldier lies on the frozen ground,
  While crack his joints with aches and ails;
A "shoddy" blanket wraps him round,
  His "shoddy" garments the wind assails.
His coat is "shoddy" well "stuffed" with "flocks;"
  He dreams of the flocks on his native hill;
His feverish sense the demon mocks—
  The demon that drives the shoddy mill.

Aye! pierce his tissues with shooting pains,
  Tear the muscles and rend the bone,
Fire with frenzy the heart and brain;
  Old rough-Shoddy, your work is done;
Never again shall the bugle-blast
  Waken the sleeper that lies so still,
His dream of home and glory past;
  Fatal 's the "work" of the shoddy mill.

Struck by "shoddy," and not by "shells,"
  And not by shot our brave ones fall;
Greed of gold the story tells,
  Drop the mantle and spread the pall.
Out on the vampyres! out on those
  Who of our life-blood take their fill!
No *meaner* "traitor" the nation knows,
  Than the greedy ghoul of the shoddy mill.

## FIGHT FOR THE NIGGER.

TUNE—*Wait for the wagon.*

I calculate of darkies we soon shall have our fill,
With Abe's Proclamaticn and the Nigger Army bill;
Who could not be a soldier for the Union to fight?
Now, Abe's made the nigger the equal of the white.
Fight for the nigger,
The sweet-scented nigger,
The woolly-headed nigger,
And the Abolition crew.

Each soldier must be loyal and his officers obey,
Tho' he lives on mouldy biscuit and fights without his pay;
If his wife at home is starving, he must not be discontent,
Tho' he waits six months for green-backs worth forty-five per cent.
Fight for the nigger, &c.

Moreover, if you're drafted, do not refuse to go,
You are equal to a nigger and can make as good a show;
And when you are in battle to the *Union* be true,
But don't forget the darkey is as good a man as you!
Fight for the gger, &c.

If ordered into battle go in without delay,
Tho' slaughtered just like cattle, it's your duty to obey;
For when old Jeff is captured, p'haps paid up you may be;
If you ain't, don't mind the money, don't you set the nigger free?
Fight for the nigger, &c.

Three-cheers for honest Abe, he will be a great man yet,
Tho' he's loaded us with taxes, and burdened us with debt;
He often tells us little jokes while pocketing our pelf,
And his last has made the nigger the equal of himself.
Fight for the nigger, &c.

Guard well the *Constitution,* the Government and laws,
To every act of Congress don't forget to give applause;
And when you meet the rebels, be sure and drive them back,
Tho' you do *enslave* the white man, you must *liberate* the black.
Fight for the nigger, &c.

---

## OLD ABE AND OLD NICK.

TUNE—"*Lord Lovel.*"

'Twas one wintry night Abe Lincoln, he lay
Resting his weary head,
Strange stories to tell, the devil appeared,
And unto Abe Lincoln he said—said—said,
And unto Abe Lincoln he said.

If you'll sell me your soul I'll make you king,
And destroy your countaree.
"It's a go," said Old Abe, almost out of breath,
A man of my word I will be—be—be,
A man of my word I will be.

Then he sent for Seward and Simon the thief,
And Welles and Bates and Blair,
To these trusty old traitors, Abe Lincoln he said,
In my new nigger kingdom you'll share—share—share,
In my new nigger kingdom you'll share.

The devil he came, and asked for his claim,
Old Abe knew not what to do;
Said the devil, make haste, I've no time to waste,
For old Nick is waiting for you—you—you,
For Old Nick is waiting for you.

---

## HOW ARE YOU, GREEN-BACKS?

We're coming, Father Abram, One hundred thousand more,
Five hundred presses printing us from morn till night is o'er;
Like magic, you will see us start and scatter thro' the land,
To pay the soldiers, or release the border Contraband
CHORUS: With our Promise to pay: How are you, Secretary Chase?
Promise to pay: Oh! dat's what's de matter.;

We're coming, Father Abram, One hundred thousand more,
And cash was ne'er so easily evok'd from rags before,
To line the fat Contractor's purse, or purchase transport craft,

Whose rotten hulks shall sink before the winds begin
to waft:
CHORUS: With our Promise to pay: How are
[you, Gideon Welles, Esquire?
Promise to pay: Oh! can't you fix the
[date?

We're coming, Father Abram, Nine hundred thousand
more,
With the greatest fighting Hero, that lives upon our
shore;
He fought in all the battles won, and shed his blood
most freely,
But he's fought them with the TRIBUNE, and his name
is Gen'l Greeley.
CHORUS: With our Promise to pay: How are
[you, Black-Brigade?
Promise to pay—Three cheers for Father
[Abe!

---

## WHEN THIS CRUEL DRAFT IS OVER.

TUNE "*When this cruel war is over.*"

Dearest love, I fear they 'll draft you,
They 'll put you on the list,
And they'll turn the wheel to grind you
Into a Lincoln grist.
CHORUS: Weeping sad and lonely,
All my tears are vain;
When this cruel draft is over,
Wilt thou come again?

O how fondly I adored you,
When you first were mine,
All the time still growing dearer,
All my soul is thine.
CHORUS: Weeping sad and lonely, &c.

But Old Abe I know will draft you,
And drag you far from me;
O, I cannot live without you,
My heart so cold will be.
CHORUS: Weeping sad and lonely, &c.,

---

## WHITE SOLDIERS' SONG.

TUNE—" *John Brown.*"

Tell Abe Lincoln that he'd better end the war,
Tell Abe Lincoln what we all came out here for,
Tell Abe Lincoln 'twas the Union to restore,
As we go marching on.—CHORUS.

Tell Abe Lincoln to let the nigger be,
Tell Abe Lincoln that we don't want him free,
Tell Abe Lincoln that to this he did agree,
As we, &c.—CHORUS.

Tell Abe Lincoln the Constitution is our guide,
Tell Abe Lincoln by the laws he must abide,
Tell Abe Lincoln to let his proclamation slide,
As we, &c.—CHORUS.

Tell Abe Lincoln and his woolly-headed crew,
Tell Abe Lincoln his suspension writ won't do,
Tell Old Abe we are going to put him through,
As we, &c.—CHORUS.

Tell Abe Lincoln of Antietam's bloody dell,
Tell Abe Lincoln where a thousand heroes fell,
Tell Abe Lincoln and his gang to go to h—l,
And we''ll go marching HOME.—CHORUS.

## PRETTY PICTURE—AIN'T IT, NEIGHBOR?

When this cruel war is over,
And our friends all crippled are,
All the nigs will be in clover,
While white trash can work and swear.
Blacks at ease—whites at labor,
Pretty picture, ain't it, neighbor?

When this cruel war is over,
Many, very many years from now,
And we the taxes then are paying,
Abe will catch it some we trow!
Blacks at ease—whites at labor,
Pretty picture, ain't it, neighbor?

When this cruel war is over,
And men in rags and debt and taxes,
The politicians will be remembered
Who used our blood to grind their axes.
Blacks at ease—whites at labor,
Figure different—can you, neighbor?

---

## DE NIGGER ON DE FENCE.

AIR—"*All around my hat.*"

Now, listen to me, white folks, de truth I'm going to tell you:
Dat de white man isn't nowhere now, it's plain to men of sense;
For, it's nigger in de Senate-house, and nigger in de White-house,
And nigger in de Custom house, and nigger on de fence.

Some time ago, when Congress met, dey spoke about de nation:
Dey made de acts, dey passed de bills, de laws dey did dispense;
And, speaking of DE PEOPLE, dey always meant de white folks:
But now in every speech dey make, de nigger 's on de fence.

Dere 's Vendell Phillips, Sumner, Horace Greeley Henry Beecher
All worshiping de nigger: fellow feeling 's deir pretences;
But dey never stop to think if dey can benefit de white man,
Dey preach and pray and talk about de nigger on de fence.

Now, just take up de TRIBUNE, and lots of oder papers,
And all de news you 'spect to read, you 'll see how dey condense;
It 's all about de slavery and abolition questions;
For, de idol dat dey worship is de nigger on de fence.

Dey try to prove de nigger am superior to de white man.
And, though dey find dat he is strong, it gives dem no offence;
For, if dey only had deir way, de Mokes should rule de nation,
And deir candidate for President be; de nigger on de fence.

Now, dere 's but one way to end de war, and save dis glorious Union,
To spare de lives of thousands, and stop de great expense:
Stand by de Constitution : no more of abolition :
And darn de man dat meddles wid de nigger on de fence!

---

## ABRAHAM THE FIRST (REPUDIATOR.)

Quoth Yankee Doodle, right away,
I hope you will, without delay,
Tell why you don't receive your pay,
Rail-splitting Abe;
For if it's true, what people say,
You're acting shabby.

From Dixie's land to Northern lake,
(It is a fact, there's no mistake,)
Greenbacks you legal tender make
'Midst all disasters;
And why do you refuse to take
Your own shinplasters?

Now, Abe, betwixt you and me,
The reason why I cannot see,
Why you, in common honesty,
Who help to make them,
The first man in the land should be
That would not take them.

You know that we are daily told
The greenbacks are as good as gold,
And why you should from them withhold
Seems rather funny,
Are you afraid of being sold
With your own money?

Admirer of the negro race,
Now don't you think it a disgrace
Unto a man in your high place
To turn his coat—
Repudiate his pretty face
On his own note ?

In after years, when men relate
The acts of Abraham the Great—
Rail splitter from Illinois State,
Chief of the Nation—
They'll say he did initiate
Repudiation.

---

## SONG OF THE "LOYAL" LEAGUERS.

We 're going to fight for darkies now,
Glory hallelujah !
At Lincoln's negro altars bow,
Glory hallelujah !

Come, jolly white men, come along,
Glory hallelujah !
Fall in, and sing this merry song,
Glory hallelujah !

O, when we get the negroes free,
Glory hallelujah !
As good as negroes we shall be,
Glory hallelujah !

—*Old Guard.*

## THE WIDOWED SWORD.

They have sent me the sword that my brave boy wore
 On the field of his young renown—
On the last red field, where his fate was sealed,
 And the sun of his days went down.
  Away with tears
   That are blinding me so;
  There is joy in his years,
   Though his young head be low;
And I'll gaze with a solemn delight evermore,
On the sword that my brave boy wore.

'Twas for freedom and home that I gave him away,
 Like the sons of his race of old;
And, though aged and gray, I am childless this day,
 He is dearer a thousand-fold.
  There's a glory above him
   To hallow his name—
  A land that will love him
   Who died for its fame;
And a solace will shine when my old heart is sore,
Round the sword that my brave boy wore.

All so noble, so true—how they stood, how they fell
 In the battle, the plague, and the cold;
Oh, as bravely and well as e'er story could tell,
 Of the flowers of the heroes of old,
  Like a sword through the foe
   Was that fearful attack,
  That so bright ere the blow
   Comes so bloodily back;
And, foremost among them his colors he bore—
And here is the sword that my brave boy wore.

It was kind of his comrades, ye know not how kind;
It is more than the Indies to me;
Ye know not how kind and how steadfast of mind
The soldier to sorrow can be.
They knew well how lonely—
How grievously wrung
Is the heart that its only
Love loses so young;
And they closed his dark eye when the battle was o'er,
And sent his old father the sword that he wore.

---

## I'M GOING TO FIGHT MIT SIGEL.

[Written by JOHN F. POOLE and sung by H. W. EGAN.]

AIR—"*The Girl I left behind me.*"

I've come shust now to tells you how
I goes mit regimentals,
To SCHLAUCH dem voes of Liberty,
Like dem old Continentals,
Vot fights mit England, long ago,
To save de Yankee Eagle;
Un now I gets mine sojer clothes,
I'm going to fight mit Sigel.
CHORUS: Yaw! daus is drue, I shpeaks mit you,
I'm going to fight mit Sigel.

Ven I comes from de Deutsche Countree,
I vorks somedimes at baking;
Den I keeps a lager bier saloon,
Un den I goes shoe-making;
But now I was a soger been
To save the Yankee Eagle;
To SCHLAUCH dem tam Secession volks,
I'm going to fight mit Sigel. CHORUS: Yaw, &c.

I gets EIN tam big rifle guns,
  Un puts him to mine shoulder,
Den march so bold, like a big jack-horse,
  Un may been someding bolder;
I goes off mit de volunteers,
  To save de Yankee Eagle;
To give dem Rebel vellers fits,
  I'm going to fight mit Sigel. CHORUS: Yaw, &c.

Dem Deutshen mens, mit Sigel's band,
  At fighting have no rival;
Un ven Cheff Davis' mens we meet,
  Ve SCHLAUCH 'em like de tuyvil,
Dere's only von ting vot I fear,
  Ven pattling for de Eagle:
I von't get not no lager bier,
  Ven I goes to fight mit Sigel. CHORUS: Yaw, &c.

For rations dey gives salty pork,
  I dinks dat was a great sell;
I petter likes de SOUR KROUT,
  De SWITZER KAISE un PRETZEL.
If Fighting Joe (or Little Mac) will give us dem;
  Ve'll save de Yankee Eagle;
Un I'll put mine VROU in breechaloons,
  To go un fight mit Sigel. CHORUS: Yaw, &c.

## GRAFTED INTO THE ARMY.

Our Jimmy has gone to live in a tent,
They have grafted him into the army;
He finally pucker'd up courage and went,
When they grafted him into the army.
I told them the child was too young: alas!
At the Captain's fore-quarters, they say, he would pass.
They'd train him up well in the infantry class—
So they grafted him into the army.

CHORUS.

O Jimmy, farewell! your brothers fell
Way down in Alabarmy;
I thought they would spare a lone widder's heir,
But they grafted him into the army.

Dressed up in his unicorn, dear little chap!
They have grafted him into the army;
It seems but a day since he sot in my lap;
But they grafted him into the army;
And these are the trousers he used to wear—
Them very same buttons—the patch and the "tear"—
But Uncle Sam gave him a bran new pair,
When they grafted him into the army.
CHORUS: O Jimmy, farewell! &c.

Now, in my provisions I see him revealed—
They have grafted him into the army;
A picket beside the contented field,
They have grafted him into the army.
He looks kinder sickish—begins to cry—
A big volunteer standing right in his eye!
Oh! what, if the ducky should up and die,
Now they've grafted him into the army!
CHORUS: O Jimmy, farewell! &c.

## MILES O'REILLY ON THE "NAYGURS."

TUNE.—*Low Backed Car.*

Some tell us 'tis a burning shame
  To make the naygurs fight;
An' that the thrade of bein' kilt
  Belongs but to the white;
But as for me, upon my sowl,
  So liberal are we here,
I'll let Sambo be murdered in place of myself
  On every day in the year!
      On every day in the year, boys,
        An' every hour in the day,
      The right to be kilt I'll divide wid him,
        An' divil a word I'll say.

In battle's wild commotion,
  I shouldn't at all object,
If Sambo's body should stop a ball
  That was coming for me direct;
An' the prod of a Southern bagnet,
  So liberal are we here,
I'll resign and let Sambo take it
  On every day in the year!
      On every day in the year, boys,
        An' wid none of your nasty pride,
      All my right in a Southern bagnet prod
        Wid Sambo I'll divide.

The men who object to Sambo
  Should take his place and fight;
An' it's better to have a naygur's hue
  Than a liver that's wake an' white;

Though Sambo's black as the ace of spades,
His finger a thrigger can pull,
An' his eye runs straight on the barrel sights
From under his thatch of wool.
So hear my all, boys, darlings,
Don't think I'm tippin' you chaff,
The right to be kilt I'll divide wid him,
An' give him the biggest half!

## WHEN THIS CRUEL DRAFT IS OVER!

Dearest William they will draft you;
They have placed your name on the list;
If you possessed a brown stone front,
Three hundred dollars wouldn't be miss'd.
CHORUS: I hope they will not draft you,
Or put your name in the wheel;
When this cruel draft is over,
Oh! how contented I will feel!

They tell me that when you are drafted,
You'll be sent to the seat of war;
Then in battle you'll be wounded,
And come home with many a scar.
CHORUS: I hope they will not draft you,
And take you away from me;
When this cruel draft is over,
Oh! how happy I will be!

If the Rebels they should kill you,
Then what would become of me?
I'm sure I'd die broken hearted,
If your face I ne're should see.
CHORUS: I hope they will not draft you,
And leave me alone to mourn,
When this cruel draft is over,
And you should ne'er more return.

## OLD ABE, MY JOLLY JO.

AIR—"*John Anderson, My Jo John.*"

Old Abraham, my jolly Abe,
  When we were first acquaint,
I thought you were an honest man,
  But nothing of a saint;
But since you wore the Spanish cloak,
  You love the negro so,
And hate the white man, so you do,
  My jolly Abe, my Jo.
Old Abraham, my jolly Abe,
  What do you really mean?
Your negro proclamation is
  A wild fanatic's dream.
The war you did begin, old Abe,
  And that you surely know;
You should have made a compromise,
  My jolly Abe, my Jo.
Old Abraham, my jolly Abe,
  Your darkey plan has failed.
Ere this you know that cruel war
  And taxes you've entailed.
In this unhappy land, old Abe,
  Is weeping, wail, and woe,
That you can't cure, nor we endure,
  My jolly Abe, my Jo.
Old Abraham, my jolly Abe,
  The blindest man can see,
The Union you will not restore
  Till every negro's free,
And equal with the best of men,
  In arm and arm they go
To vote as you may wish them to,
  My jolly Abe, my Joe.

## THE CONSCRIPT'S HYMN.

TUNE—" *Windham.*"

Well may we mourn, conscripted friends,
And shake at draft's alarms,
For 'tis the voice that Old Abe sends
To make us shoulder arms.

To make us fight for darkies black,
And shed our blood like rain—
We startle at the whip's sharp crack,
And wear our master's chain.

Equality is now achieved,
The white man and the black,
Of God's distinctive mark relieved,
March on a common track.

Then on, conscripted martyrs go,
To do Abe's bloody will,
Lay every white man's body low,
With blacks his mansions fill.

Go on to murder, steal and burn,
To pillage field and plain,
The white man's home to ruin turn,
With blood his altars stain!

O give the darkey freedom's boon,
But take the white man's breath,
A nation's sun goes down at noon,
Draped in the shrouds of death.

## THE FLAG OF DEMOCRACY.

TUNE—" *Star-Spangled Banner.*"

Oh! say can you see, through the gloom and the storm,
More bright for the darkness, that pure constellation?
Like the symbol of love and redemption its form,
As it points to the haven of hope for the nation.
How radiant each star, as the beacon afar,
Giving promise of peace, and an end of the war!
'Tis Democracy's Flag, which shall ever remain
To light us to freedom and glory again!

How peaceful and blest was America's soil
'Till betray'd by the guile of the Puritan demon,
Which lurks under Virtue, and springs from its coil
To fasten its fangs in the life-blood of freemen.
Then boldly appeal to each heart that can feel,
And crush the foul viper 'neath Liberty's heel!
And Democracy's Flag shall in triumph remain
To light us to freedom and glory again!

'T is the emblem of peace, 't is the day star of hope,
Like the sacred *Labarum* that guided the Roman;
From the shore of the Gulf to Maine's rocky slope,
'T is the trust of the free and the terror of foemen.
Fling its folds to the air, while we boldly declare,
The rights we demand or the deeds that we dare!
While Democracy's Flag shall in triumph remain
To light us to freedom and glory again!

And if peace should be hopeless and justice denied,
And war's bloody vulture should flap its black pinions,
Then gladly "*to arms*," while we hurl in our pride,
Defiance to *tyrants* and death to their minions!
With our front in the field, swearing *never to yield*,
Or return like the Spartan in death on our shield!
And Democracy's Flag shall triumphantly wave
O'er the land of the free or the pall of the brave!

## WHEN THIS CRUEL WAR IS OVER.

[Words by CHA'S CARROLL SAWYER—Music by HENRY TUCKER.—Music of this song for sale by SAWYER & THOMPSON, Publishers, 59 Fulton Avenue, Brooklyn, N. Y.]

Dearest love, do you remember
  When we last did meet,
How you told me that you loved me,
  Kneeling at my feet?
Oh! how proud you stood before me,
  In your suit of blue,
When you vow'd to be and Country,
  Ever to be true.
        Weeping, sad and lonely,
          Hopes and fears, how vain:
        Yet praying, when this cruel war is over,
          Praying: that we meet again!

When the summer breeze is sighing,
  Mournfully, along!
Or when Autumn leaves are falling,
  Sadly breathes the song,
Oft, in dreams, I see thee lying
  On the battle plain,
Lonely, wounded, even dying:
  Calling, but in vain—
        Weeeping, sad and lonely, &c.

If, amid the din of battle,
  Nobly you should fall,
Far away from those who love you,
  None to hear you call:
Who would whisper words of comfort,
  Who would soothe your pain?
Ah! the many cruel fancies
  Ever in my brain—
        Weeping, sad and lonely, &c.

But our Country called you, darling,
Angels cheer your way;
While our nation's sons are fighting,
We can only pray.
Nobly strike for God and Liberty,
Let all nations see
How we love our Starry Banner,
Emblem of the free!—
Weeping, sad and lonely, &c.

---

## PARODY ON WHEN THIS CRUEL WAR IS OVER.

Och, Biddy dear, do you remember
Whin we last did meet?
'Twas at Paddy Murphy's party,
Down in Baxter street;
And there, all the boys did envy me,
And girls envy'd you—
Whin they saw my great big bounty
In Green-Backs, all new!
CHORUS: Och, weepin', Biddy darlin',
For the Pay-Master's tin;
When this cruel war is over,
Praying—for a good horn of gin.

Next day, I shoulder'd my ould musket,
Braver thin Ould Mars;
And, with spirits light and airy,
Marched off to the wars;
But now me drame of glory 's over,
I'm homesick, I fear;
I'd give this world for a substitute,
To take my place here. CHORUS.

Och, Biddy darlin', things are changing,
  Since I left New York;
There, I got good beef-steak plenty—
  Now I get salt pork;
And the crackers, Biddy jewel,
  For to tell the truth,
They are harder than a brick-bat,
  And wud break yer tooth. CHORUS.

Whin the cabbages are blooming,
  Beautiful and strong;
Or whin whiskey-punch is brewin'—
  Mournful is my song;
In me drames, I often see ye walking
  With that big black-guard Tim;
Oh! if I could only get a furlough,
  Would'nt I slather him! CHORUS.

---

## DEAR MOTHER, I'VE COME HOME TO DIE.

Dear Mother, I remember well
  The parting kiss you gave to me,
When merry rang the village bell;
  My heart was full of joy and glee;
I did not dream that one short year
  Would crush the hopes that soar'd so high!
Oh! Mother dear, draw near to me,
  Dear Mother, I've come home to die.

CHORUS:

Call sister—brother—to my side,
And take your soldier's last good-bye,
Good-bye;
Oh! Mother dear, draw near to me,
Dear Mother, I've come home to die.

Hark!—Mother, 'tis the village bell—
  I can no longer with you stay:
My Country calls—to arms! to arms!
  The foe advance in fierce array!
The vision's past—I feel that now
  For country I can only sigh:
Oh! Mother dear, draw near to me,
  Dear Mother, I've come home to die.
    CHORUS: Call sister, &c.

Dear Mother, Sister, Brother, all—
  One parting kiss—to all: Good-bye!
Weep not! but clasp your hand in mine,
  And let me like a soldier die!
I've met the foe upon the field,
  Where kindred fiercely did defy—
I fought for Right—God bless the Flag!
  Dear Mother, I've come home to die!
    CHORUS: Call sister, &c.

---

## OUR DEAD.

Wrap the starry banner round him;
  Comrades, gently lay him low,
Breathe a mournful dirge above him,
  Softly, sadly, ere we go!

To and fro the pine trees swaying,
  Bend with reverence to the grave,
Seem to chant, amid their sighing,
  Mournful requiems for the brave.

Wrap the flag he swore to cherish
  Round his noble manly form;
Sad, that one like him should perish
  In the first burst of the storm.

For our country needs such spirits
  To sustain her till the end;
And bring back those erring children
  Who have sworn our land to rend.

As of old the Christian Martyrs,
  Go these young hearts to the strife,
Sacrifice to love of country
  All that they hold dear in life.

'Mid our tears and great affliction,
  Feel we that they from above,
Like the ancient christian heroes,
  Still watch o'er the cause they love.

Let us leave him, comrades! sleeping
  In this Southern forest dim;
While tall pines their watch are keeping,
  Standing guardians over him.

---

## SONG OF GREENBACKS.

AIR.—"*Sing a Song of Sixpence.*"

Sing a song of greenbacks,
  A pocket full of trash,
Over head and ears in debt,
  And out of ready cash;

Heaps of tax collectors,
  As busy as a bee;
Ain't we in a pretty fix
  With gold at fifty-three.

Abe in the White House
  Proclamations printing;
Meade on the Rapidan
  Afraid to do the fighting;
Seward in the Cabinet
  Surrounded by his spies;
Halleck with the telegraph
  Busy forging lies.

Chase in the Treasury
  Making worthless notes;
Curtin at Harrisburg
  Making shoddy coats;
Dahlgren at Charleston
  Lost in a fog;
Forney under Abe's chair
  Barking like a dog.

Schenck down at Baltimore
  Doing dirty work;
Butler at Norfolk
  As savage as a Turk;
Sprague in Rhode Island
  Eating apple sass;
Everett at Gettysburg
  Talking like an ass;

Banks out in Texas
  Trying to cut a figure;
Beecher in Brooklyn
  Howling for the nigger;

Lots of Abolitionists
Kicking up a yell,
In comes Parson Brownlow
And sends them all to hell;

Burnside at Knoxville
In a kind of fix;
Gilmore at Sumter
Pounding at the bricks;
Grant at Chattanooga
Trying Bragg to thrash;
Is it any wonder
The Union's gone to smash?

---

## THE WASTE OF WAR.

Give me the gold that war has cost,
Before this peace-expanding day,
The wasted skill the labor lost—
The mental treasure thrown away;
And I will buy each rood of soil
In every yet discovered land;
Where hunters roam, where peasants toil,
Where many peopled cities stand.

I'll clothe each shivering wretch on earth,
In needful, aye, in brave attire;
Vesture befitting banquet mirth
Which kings might envy and admire,
In every vale, on every plain,
A school shall glad the gazer's sight,
Where every poor man's child may gain
Pure knowledge, free as air and light.

I'll build asylums for the poor,
  By age or ailment made forlorn;
And none shall thrust them from the door,
  Or sting with looks and words of scorn.
I'll link each alien hemisphere;
  Help honest men to conquer wrong;
Art, Science, Labor, nerve and cheer,
  Reward the Poet for his song.

In every free and peopled clime,
  A vast Walhalla hall shall stand;
A marble edifice sublime,
  For the illustrious of the land;
A Pantheon for the truly great,
  The wise, beneficient and just;
A place of wide and lofty state
  To honor and to hold their dust.

---

## SONG OF THE BLACKSMITH'S WIFE.

AIR.—"*The Maid of Llangollen.*"

My husband's a blacksmith, and where will you find
A man more industrious, faithful, and kind?
He's determined to thrive, and in that we agree,
For the ring of his anvil is music to me.

Though dark his complexion and grimy his shirt,
Hard and horny his hand, and disfigured with dirt;
Yet in that rude casket a jewel I see,
And the ring of his anvil is music to me.

Ere Aurora's fair nymphs chase the night from the
skies,
Ere the sun pierce the glooming, from bed he does
rise,
Ere the lark leaves her nest, at his forge he will be,
And the ring of his anvil is music to me.

Though to labor he owns, we are far from being poor,
Industry has banished gaunt Want from our door;
For the blacksmith's a man independent and free,
And the ring of his anvil is music to me.

At a distance from home I have seen with delight
The red sparks from his chimney illumine the night,
And have heard the fast strokes on the anvil rebound,
And my heart has leaped up at the musical sound.

Those strokes on the anvil, say what do they prove?
Forethought and affection, industry and love;
A resolve to be honest, respected, and free!
That's the tune on the anvil that's music to me.

www.ingramcontent.com/pod-product-compliance
Lightning Source LLC
LaVergne TN
LVHW021428110826
845150LV00007B/2133

* 9 7 8 1 4 2 5 5 0 8 2 7 2 *